5/11   l.e. 3/16

D1541659

Write It Out:

Mastering Short and Extended Responses to Open-Ended Questions, Level E

Coach™
America's Best for Student Success®

Triumph Learning®

A Haights Cross Communications ® Company

About the Authors

Sheila Crowell and **Ellen Kolba** are specialists in the teaching of writing and in preparing students for writing assessments. Their textbooks provide the affirmative support and scaffolding all students need to become better, more confident writers and to improve their scores on writing assessments.

As staff developers and writing curriculum specialists, Crowell and Kolba show teachers how to evaluate writing by first identifying and specifying the strengths in a draft, and then making suggestions based on those strengths to prompt revision. To support the teaching of writing in their own school district in Montclair, New Jersey, they developed **The Writers' Room**™ program, which trains volunteers from the community, pre-service teachers, and students to serve as writing coaches in elementary, middle, and high school language arts and English classes.

Under their direction, **The Writers Room** program has been brought to schools in Elizabeth, Metuchen, and Trenton, New Jersey, as well as to districts in New York, California, and Canada.

Acknowledgments

Special thanks to our writing team for their help with this book:

Caleb E. Crowell

Derek Kipp

Jessica Wade

Write It Out: Mastering Short and Extended Responses to Open-Ended Questions, Level E
127NA
ISBN-10: 1-59823-028-X
ISBN-13: 978-1-59823-028-4

Cover Image: Julie Delton/Photodisc/Green/Getty Images

Triumph Learning® 136 Madison Avenue, 7th Floor, New York, NY 10016
Kevin McAliley, President and Chief Executive Officer

Printed in the United States of America.

10 9 8

Part A: Writing Short Answers

Table of Contents

Part B: Writing Extended Answers

Table of Contents

6

In school, you have to take lots of tests.

Many test questions give you a choice of answers. You must pick the correct answer from a list of choices. Questions like these are called **multiple-choice questions**.

Another type of test question asks you to write something in your own words. Questions like these, which ask you to write your own answers instead of choosing from a multiple-choice list, are often called **open-ended questions**. They might also be called **constructed-response** or **extended-response questions**. This book is about these kinds of questions.

Open-ended questions are important! An open-ended question counts for more on a test than a multiple-choice question does. So it's important to learn how to write good answers to this kind of question.

Your score on an open-ended question depends on two things:

    1) How well you understood the reading selection.

    2) How well you expressed your answer in writing.

This book will give you practice doing both.

An open-ended question may call for a short answer or an extended answer.

  A short answer contains only a few sentences or a paragraph.

  An extended answer may take two paragraphs or more—even a page.

In this book, you will practice writing both short and extended responses to open-ended questions. By the time you get to the end of the book, you should be ready to handle most open-ended questions on a real test.

So let's get started!

5 Rules for Writing Good Answers

Open-ended questions are based on a reading selection. When taking such a test, you first need to read the selection, then answer the questions that follow. So in order to practice answering open-ended questions, you need to start with a reading selection.

When you turn the page, you'll see a selection for you to read. Read it carefully. All the questions in the rest of this introduction are about this selection. You may read the selection as many times as you like if you need help to answer the questions.

This introduction will also show you five rules for writing good answers. We call these rules the **SLAMS** rules. Note the underlined letter in each rule. At the end of the introduction, you'll see why.

Now turn the page to begin reading the selection.

8

Big Wing

What migrates south for the winter, sings beautiful songs, and has a scientific name that means "big wing"? It must be some kind of bird, right?

Not exactly. For starters, this animal weighs about 90,000 pounds. It also lives in the ocean, and it gives birth to live babies. The only bird that spends a lot of time in the ocean is a penguin, and penguins do not weigh 90,000 pounds! Also, baby birds hatch from eggs, so this animal is definitely not a bird.

Do you give up? It's a whale—the Pacific humpback whale, to be exact. In the summer, these whales live and feast in the ocean near Alaska. In the winter, they swim 5,000 miles to Hawaii to give birth and attract new mates. Strangely enough, the whales never eat anything while they are there.

Humpback whales are big, clunky creatures. Imagine a creature the size of six SUV's parked side by side, and you get the idea. A big humpback can weigh more than 45 tons—about the weight of 10,000 fifth graders.

It takes a lot of food to build a body that big. Fortunately, the waters near Alaska are filled with the small fish and shrimp that form the humpback's diet.

To get its food, a humpback often blows "bubble nets" by swimming in a circle underwater and blowing blasts of bubbles from its blowhole. The bubbles scare the fish into a tightly packed group. The whale then opens its huge mouth and gulps in the fish—along with a lot of ocean water. With its tongue, the whale forces the water out through long, bristly bones in its mouth called baleen. The fish remain trapped, and the whale has a perfect meal. Humpbacks do not have teeth, so the fish and shrimp are swallowed whole.

After a summer of eating in Alaska, the humpbacks begin their long migration south. It's the longest migration made by any mammal. They swim slowly—only about three miles an hour, or about as fast as you walk. At that speed, it takes them two months or more to make the trip to Hawaii. By late autumn, they are living in the sunny waters off the coast of the Hawaiian island of Maui.

There, the pregnant females give birth to their babies, while the unattached females are courted by male humpbacks. The babies feed on their mother's milk, but the adult whales never eat. They live off the stored fat from their summer feasting.

In spite of their bulk and slowness, humpbacks are the most athletic of all whales. They love to leap out of the water, often spinning or turning somersaults and landing on their backs with an immense splash. They whack the water with their huge front flippers, which may be twenty feet long. It's these flippers that caused scientists to give humpbacks the scientific name Megaptera, which means "big wing."

Humpback males also sing. They combine trills, chirps, deep moans, and whistles into surprisingly beautiful underwater songs. These songs may go on as long as fifteen minutes. Nobody is sure why male whales sing. Maybe they are trying to attract females. Maybe they want to threaten other males and keep them from their mates. Or maybe they sing for both reasons. In any case, their songs and antics attract thousands of human tourists, who watch them from whale-watching tour boats.

By the end of winter, the whales are getting hungry. The babies are big enough to make the long journey north. The group leaves Hawaii and swims back to Alaska to begin another summer of feeding and fattening up for next year's migration.

Rule 1: Sentences

Here is an open-ended question you might find on a test:

The selection tells about a whale that is like a bird in some ways. What is one thing that the whale does that is like a bird?

Franklin's Answer:

sings

Franklin's answer is correct. Birds sing, and so do humpback whales. But Franklin's answer probably would not get a top score. It's not a sentence.

Franklin's answer would have been better if he had written it like this:

Male humpback whales sing songs, just like some birds do.

Tell something else that humpback whales do that some birds also do.

Here is another open-ended question:

Selene's Answer:

migrate

Rewrite Selene's answer so that it would get a better score.

Rule 1

Answers to open-ended questions should always be written in complete sentences! (Exception: When you fill out a chart.)

_____

_____

_____

_____

When writing the answer to an open-ended question, it's sometimes hard to know how long your answer should be. Here's a rule to help you know:

✓ If your handwriting is big, you'll take about one-and-a-half lines to write a sentence. If you write small, you'll need only one line for a sentence.

✓ So, if you see three or four lines, you probably should write at least three sentences.

✓ If you see a whole page of lines, you probably should write at least two paragraphs. If you see two whole pages of lines, then you should write at least three paragraphs, maybe more.

Rule 2

The number of lines on the test gives you a good idea about how long your answer should be.

Justin read this question on a test:

How do humpback whales catch fish?

Justin's Answer:

Humpbacks use bubbles to catch fish.

_____

_____

_____

_____

_____

Can you figure out what Justin did wrong? Justin's sentence is correct, but his answer is too short. It doesn't fill up enough of the lines. He should add more details from the selection.

On the lines after Justin's answer, add more details about how humpback whales use bubbles to catch fish. Remember to write in complete sentences.

Rule 3: <u>A</u>nswer the Question

12

Many students get into trouble because they forget what the question asks. They write about a similar topic, but they don't actually answer the question. You must read the question carefully, and you must give information that belongs with the answer. For example, read this question:

> **How can the whales live in the winter if they don't eat?**

Shawn's Answer:

The whales don't eat when they are in Hawaii. They play, sing songs, have babies, and mate.

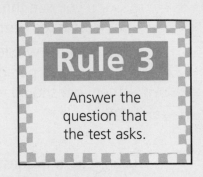

Rule 3

Answer the question that the test asks.

Nidia's Answer:

Whales don't need to eat when they are in Hawaii in the winter. They live off the fat that they build up in the summer when they eat lots of fish in Alaska.

> **What do humpback whales do that makes people say that the whales are athletic?**

The information in both answers is true. But Shawn's answer is not a good one. ***He did not answer what the question asks.***

✓ The question doesn't ask what whales do when they are in Hawaii. It asks how the whales survive if they don't eat during the winter.

Nidia's answer is much better. She answers the question that was asked.

Try it. Answer this question, using the information in the selection:

_____

_____

_____

_____

_____

_____

Rule 4: <u>M</u>echanics Count

When writers—or teachers—talk about "mechanics," they don't mean people who fix things. In writing, mechanics means spelling, punctuation, and capitalization. Mechanics also means correct grammar and proper word usage.

If you write a good answer with a few small mistakes in spelling or punctuation, you will not get a low score. But if you make several sloppy or careless mistakes, you will lose points.

Read the question and then read Julio's answer.

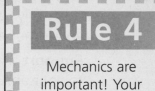

Rule 4

Mechanics are important! Your sentences should have no mistakes.

Humpbacks have no teeth. How can they eat fish?

Julio's Answer:

Humpacks eat only small fish they open their mouthes and take in both water and fish. Then they close their mouthes. And use their tongs to push water out the side's of their mouth. then they swalow the fish hole

What do you notice? Julio's answer has a lot of supporting details, but it would not get a high score. Julio did not pay attention to mechanics. His answer has the following errors:

✓ 6 spelling mistakes (1 word is misspelled twice)

✓ 1 run-on sentence and 1 incomplete sentence (a fragment)

✓ 3 mistakes in capitalization (1 because of the run-on and 1 because of the fragment)

✓ 1 mistake with apostrophes (an apostrophe that doesn't belong)

✓ 2 missing periods (1 because of the run-on sentence)

Rewrite Julio's answer with no mistakes. (HINT: All the misspelled words are spelled correctly in the selection.)

_____

_____

_____

_____

14 — Rule 5: Support Your Answers

This is probably the most important rule of all. Many students do poorly because they don't pay enough attention to it. If you forget everything else, remember this rule!

Support means to include information that explains or adds to your answer.

✓ For some questions, some or all of the support must come from the selection.

✓ For other questions, it is okay to add your own opinions, but you MUST include some information from the selection, no matter what you write.

For example, read the question and the answers that follow.

Rule 5

Support your answers with details from the selection.

> **Why do male whales sing? Support your answer with details from the selection.**

Rita's Answer:

I think that whales sing because they like the sound of their own voices and because they think that it's fun to sing. Maybe they sing because they enjoy showing off for all the tourists who come to watch them.

Courtney's Answer:

Male whales may sing to attract female whales. Maybe they also sing to warn off other males. It's like saying, "Listen to how powerful my singing is. Don't mess with me. Don't even think of coming near my mates."

Did Rita do a good job explaining why male whales sing? ___ **Yes** ___ **No**

Did Courtney do a good job explaining why
male whales sing? ___ **Yes** ___ **No**

Below are details that Rita and Courtney wrote. Check which ones are supported by information in the selection and which ones are not.

Rita:

Whales like the sound of their own voices.

___**supported by the selection** ___**NOT supported by the selection**

Whales think it's fun to sing.

___**supported by the selection** ___**NOT supported by the selection**

Whales like showing off for tourists.

___**supported by the selection** ___**NOT supported by the selection**

Courtney:

Male whales may sing to attract females.

___**supported by the selection** ___**NOT supported by the selection**

Male whales may sing to warn off other males.

___**supported by the selection** ___**NOT supported by the selection**

Male whales may be saying, "Don't even think of coming near my mates."

___**supported by the selection** ___**NOT supported by the selection**

Try it. Answer the following question. Be sure to look back at the selection for the details to support your answer.

What kind of a swimmer is the humpback whale?

_____

_____

_____

_____

_____

_____

SLAMS—A Memory Gem

To help you remember the five rules in this chapter, remember this word: SLAMS!

 stands for **S**entence. Write your answers in complete sentences.

 stands for **L**ines. The number of lines on the answer sheet gives you an idea of how long your answer should be.

 stands for **A**nswer. Answer the question that the test asks. Answer all parts of the question. Read the question a few times to make sure you understand what the question asks.

 stands for **M**echanics. Mechanics are punctuation, capitalization, spelling, grammar, and usage. Your sentence mechanics should be correct. You should write without mistakes.

 stands for **S**upport. Remember to support your answer with details from the selection.

When you answer open-ended questions, try to recall this memory gem. Give your answers the *SLAMS* test. If your answer doesn't follow all of the *SLAMS* rules, fix it!

Remember—a good answer **SLAMS** the question!

Scoring Rubric

Every test has a different way of scoring the answers to an open-ended question. One of the most common methods is a scale of **0 to 4**. The **highest score is a 4**; the **lowest score is 0.**

It might help if you know what you need to get a **4** or a **3**. Here are some rubric guidelines for answering open-ended questions.

SCORE **WHAT IT MEANS**

You answered the question clearly and completely.

You included ideas from the reading selection that are on target.

You supported these ideas with details and examples.

If the question asked you to, you connected the ideas from the reading selection to your own ideas and experiences.

You answered in complete and interesting sentences.

SCORE **WHAT IT MEANS**

You answered the question.

You included some ideas from the reading selection.

You used some examples and details for support.

If the question asked you to, you connected some of the ideas from the reading selection to your own experiences.

Most of your sentences were complete.

SCORE **WHAT IT MEANS**

You only answered part of the question.

You only included one or two ideas or details from the reading selection. The main ideas may not have been included.

You didn't connect your own ideas or experiences with the reading passage.

Many of your sentences were written incorrectly.

SCORE **WHAT IT MEANS**

You didn't seem to understand the reading selection.

Your answer didn't include the important details from the selection.

You didn't connect your ideas to the reading passage.

You often wrote only single words or groups of words instead of complete sentences.

SCORE **WHAT IT MEANS**

You didn't write anything; OR

You didn't answer the question asked.

Part A

Writing Short Answers

Main Idea and Supporting Details

When you read, you don't just read individual words. You try to understand the thoughts and ideas that the words express. You look for the **main idea** behind what you read, or what the whole thing is all about.

For example, suppose someone asks you what the book and movie series *The Lord of the Rings* is about. You could say something like this:

> *It's about a little Hobbit named Frodo, who has to destroy an evil magic ring by throwing it back into the volcano where it was made. If the Dark Lord Sauron gets it back before Frodo and his friends can destroy it, he will take over the world.*

Notice the details in this description of the main idea:

- the Hobbit's name;

- what kind of ring he has to destroy;

- what will happen if he doesn't destroy it.

Often when a question asks you to identify the main idea, it also asks you to include **supporting details**.

On the next page, you will read a short informational passage. The question that follows the selection asks you to identify the selection's main idea and supporting details.

22

Lesson 1

What Makes a Good Answer?

Read this informational passage. The question on the next page asks you to identify the main idea and the supporting details.

Pictures in the Sky

The next time you go out at night in the fall, look toward the north. There, hanging low in the sky, sparkles a group of stars that look like the picture on this page. You can easily see them if the skies are clear and the street lights aren't too bright.

The main idea is expressed in this paragraph.

Throughout history, people have always "connected the dots" to make pictures out of groups of stars. Around the world, people have given these groupings different names. For example, to people who live in the United States, one star grouping looks like a long-handled dipper that people once used to scoop drinking water out of a well. About two hundred years ago they started calling it the Big Dipper. We still call it that today, even though we don't use dippers much anymore.

However, not everyone around the world identified this star grouping as a "big dipper." People who live in the south of France think these stars look like a saucepan, which is not very different from a dipper. People in Britain look at these stars and see an old-fashioned plow or a wagon. The four stars in front, which are the bowl of the Big Dipper, make up the wagon's body. The rest of the stars, which are the handle of the Big Dipper, create the pole to which horses or oxen are hitched to the wagon.

These paragraphs are loaded with supporting details.

The ancient Egyptians looked at these stars and saw the leg of a bull. The ancient Greeks looked at the stars and saw a giant bear with a long tail. Some Native Americans of the Plains saw a skunk, while the Maya Native Americans of Mexico saw a long-tailed parrot.

What picture do you see in these stars? What picture do you imagine as you connect the dots?

What is the main idea of the passage? Support your answer with details from the passage.

Melissa's Answer:

One way to learn how to write a good answer is to analyze a good answer that someone has written. Melissa wrote a good answer to this question. Read what she wrote.

> The main idea of this passage is that different people who look at the stars in the Big Dipper see different things. For example, Americans see a dipper. However, the British see a wagon. The ancient Greeks saw a bear, and different Native American people saw a skunk or a parrot.

What Makes Melissa's Answer Work?

Melissa does what the test scorers look for:

✓ She summarizes the main idea.

✓ She mentions a few details that support the main idea.

✓ She writes clear, complete sentences and arranges them in an order that makes sense.

✓ She demonstrates that she has read both the question and the reading selection very carefully.

✓ She remembers the SLAMS rules!

HINT!

The people who score the test look for the following things:

* A clear and complete sentence that tells the main idea.

* Details from the selection that support your first sentence.

* Complete, correct, and interesting sentences.

Now let's take a closer look at Melissa's answer to see why it is successful.

1. Melissa states the main idea of the passage.

   What is Melissa's main idea? Write her main-idea sentence here.

   _____

   _____

   _____

2. In her answer, Melissa includes details from the passage that support the main idea. One detail tells what Americans see in these stars.

   a. **In which sentence does Melissa include this detail? Write Melissa's sentence here.**

   _____

   _____

   _____

   b. **Find another supporting detail that Melissa includes in her answer. Write the sentence in which Melissa gives that detail here.**

   _____

   _____

   _____

3. One reason that Melissa's answer is so clear and easy to understand is that she uses words like *for example* to connect ideas.

   Find another connecting word that Melissa uses. Write the sentence with that word here.

   _____

   _____

   _____

Tools & Tips

You explored several reasons why Melissa's answer worked. One reason was that she used words like **for example** to connect her ideas. Another reason is that she connected ideas by combining sentences. Here is an example from her answer:

> *The ancient Greeks saw a bear, and different Native American people saw a skunk or a parrot.*

How many ideas have been combined in this sentence? Two ideas have been listed below. Finish the list.

The ancient Greeks saw a bear.

Some Native American people saw a skunk.

_____

_____

Try it. Combine the ideas below into one sentence. Notice that you can combine the ideas in more ways than one.

> *This group of stars looked like a dipper. They looked like a dipper with a long handle. People used these dippers to scoop water out of a well.*

Write your combined sentence here.

_____

_____

_____

_____

Lesson 2

Revising and Improving a Weak Answer

Here is another reading selection about stars. The question on the next page asks you to identify the main idea.

The Guide to the North

Imagine that you are in a boat in the middle of the ocean. The nearest land is a low-lying island thirty miles to the north. You can't see it, but you know it's there. You're running out of water, and your goal is to land on that island and hope it has a fresh mountain stream. The problem is that you don't have a compass. How do you know which way is north?

Find one supporting detail in this paragraph.

The task isn't as difficult as it sounds. In fact, long ago, mariners did not have the modern tools we have today. Instead, they knew that one star in the night sky always sat in a northward position. They used this star to guide their ships. You can use it, too.

The main idea is expressed in this paragraph.

To find that star, let the Big Dipper be your guide. Do you see the two stars that form the front of the bowl? These stars are the pointer stars. Imagine a line connecting the pointer stars, starting at the bottom of the bowl and going up and "out" of the bowl. Continue the line until you come to another star. It will be about five times the distance between the pointer stars. This star is the North Star, also called Polaris. It may not be the brightest star in the night sky, but it has another special feature—it always hangs over the North Pole. It never changes position. So if you can find this star, you always know which way is north.

More than 150 years ago, African American slaves used the Big Dipper to help them escape from slavery and head north. They called the Big Dipper "the Drinking Gourd," and they knew that if they walked toward it, they would be walking northward. Eventually they would reach freedom. The North Star has been guiding people, both on land and at sea, for centuries.

How could you best summarize this passage in two or three sentences?

Luis tried to answer this question, but he wasn't successful. Figure out what Luis needs to improve his answer.

Luis's Answer:

The dipper points to the north. If an island is north of you.

Improving Luis's Answer

Luis's answer would not a get a good score because it is a partial answer. He has stated one important fact—that the Big Dipper can be used to find north. He has included one detail as well. However, his answer is very short, and he doesn't always use complete sentences. The passage contains important details about finding north that Luis has not included, and the detail about the island is not very important at all.

How could Luis improve his answer? Use the questions on this page and the next page to help you revise and improve Luis's answer.

1. Did Luis state the most important fact about the part of the Big Dipper that can be used to find north?

   If not, what sentence should Luis write to start his answer? Write the new sentence here.

   _____

   _____

   _____

   _____

   _____

HINT!

Test scorers look for the following things:

* A clear and complete statement of the main idea.

* Details from the selection that support the main idea.

* Complete, correct, and interesting sentences.

2. You have explained what part of the Big Dipper can be used to find north.
What details from the selection should you add to support and complete the main idea? Write the new sentence or sentences here.

_____

_____

_____

3. Which detail in Luis's original summary doesn't belong?
   a. **Write the sentence Luis should take out here.**

_____

_____

   b. **What other detail from the selection could Luis include in his summary? Write it here.**

_____

_____

_____

4. **Now rewrite Luis's answer for him on the lines below.**

_____

_____

_____

_____

_____

_____

_____

_____

_____

SCORE BUILDER

Before you forget—

What is the memory gem word?

_____

What does each letter stand for?

1 _____
_____

2 _____
_____

3 _____
_____

4 _____
_____

5 _____
_____

30

Lesson 3

Responding on Your Own

Here is a third reading selection. The question that follows asks you to explain the main idea. This time you will write the answer on you own.

The Moving Dipper

Look for the main idea in this paragraph.

The Big Dipper, like all star patterns in the sky, is always moving. Every 24 hours the Big Dipper makes a big counterclockwise circle around the North Star. On an autumn evening, about an hour after sunset, the Big Dipper sits low in the sky. By morning, 12 hours later, it will be high in the sky above the North Star, and it will appear upside down!

The Big Dipper hasn't really moved, of course. The Earth has moved, turning on its axis. The Earth's movement makes the Dipper (and all the other stars) seem to move around the sky. The sun doesn't move across the sky during the day, right? Well, the stars don't move across the sky at night either. It just looks that way!

Look for supporting details in this paragraph.

The Dipper changes positions during the year, too. On an early spring evening, it appears high in the sky and upside down. It looks just as it does before sunrise in the autumn. In the summer, the Big Dipper hangs down by its handle, and in the winter it stands on the end of its handle.

Of course, all these changes are caused by the movement of the Earth. In fact, everything in the universe moves and changes, even the stars. All the stars in the Big Dipper are moving, but we are so far away from them that they seem to be standing still. Nevertheless, a hundred thousand years from now, the Big Dipper probably will have changed its shape. In its place will be something that people might call the "Big Snake" or "The Big Upside-Down Frying Pan." The stars of the Big Dipper will probably still exist, but they will have moved in different directions to form a new pattern for people of the future to name.

Tell what this selection is mainly about. Support your answer with details from the selection.

Write your answer on the lines below.

_____

_____

_____

_____

_____

_____

_____

_____

_____

_____

_____

_____

_____

_____

_____

_____

_____

_____

_____

HINT!

When you are finished writing, check your answer:

* Is your main idea clearly stated?

* Have you supported the main idea with details from the selection?

* Does your answer meet all of the SLAMS tests?

Reader's Response!
Revise & Edit

When you have finished writing, exchange papers with a partner. As you read each other's work, answer the questions below.

1 Did the writer answer the question? ___Yes ___ No

2 Is the main idea clearly stated? ___ Yes ___ No
If not, what needs to be made clearer?
Write your response here.

_____

_____

_____

3 Are there enough details to support the main idea? ___ Yes ___ No
If not, what needs to be made clearer?
Write your response here.

_____

_____

_____

4 Has the writer followed all the SLAMS rules? ___ Yes ___ No
If not, which rule or rules were not followed?
Check all the boxes that apply.

S ___   L ___   A ___   M ___   S ___

5 **Give the paper back to your partner to revise and edit.**

Reviewing the Question

On reading tests, you often have to show that you understand the main idea of a story, an informational passage, or even a single paragraph. Questions about the main idea may be asked in different ways. Pay special attention to the words in **dark** type.

- What is the **main idea** of this selection?

- What is this selection **mostly about**?

- In a few sentences, **summarize** what you have just read.

- What is a **good title** for this selection?

Questions about the supporting details may be asked in different ways, too. Here are some of them. Pay special attention to the words in **dark** type.

- Use **details from the story** in your answer.

- Use **information from the selection** to explain your answer.

- Support your **main idea** with **details** from the selection.

Understanding Characters

Stories contain many clues about what characters are like and how they feel. Looking for these clues helps the reader understand the characters. For example, you might read a story that starts with this sentence:

Rob shoved the screen door open and walked into the kitchen, then he slammed his math book down on the table.

From just this sentence you would be able to conclude that Rob is angry or upset about something. He might be upset about his math class, but you would have to read the rest of the story to find out.

Understanding characters requires you to "read between the lines" in a story. When you read, you need to ask questions to help you understand what a character is like or how the character feels. For example:

- What do the character's actions tell me about the character's feelings?

- What do the character's words tell me about his or her feelings?

- When the author describes a character's facial expression or tone of voice, what does this tell me about the character's feelings?

Lesson 4

What Makes a Good Answer?

Here is the first part of a story. The question on the next page asks you to describe the character's feelings.

Carmen's First Day

"Ouch," I muttered to myself as my ankle twisted. I paused on the field and watched as a tall dark-haired girl sprinted past me. Expertly, she dribbled the soccer ball, coming up fast on our fullback. I limped forward as quickly as possible to assist, but it was no use. The girl dodged around our fullback, kicked, and—**_swoosh!_**—the ball hit the back of the net.

I couldn't believe how badly I was playing. I hung my head as I left the field. I wasn't good enough to stop anyone today.

That night, I iced my ankle and wondered what I was going to do. This had been my first day at Great Falls Soccer Camp, and I'd been looking forward to it all summer. I'd read in the brochure how campers got to "play soccer with college-level coaches and meet professional players." It sounded awesome. My parents said I could attend the camp, so I'd signed up for the advanced group. After all, I've been playing soccer since I was six years old, and I'm on the traveling team for 10- to 12-year-olds in my town. When I play with my team at home, I'm confident. I've known all the girls since I was six, and I know that I can play great soccer with them.

Things were different with the new girls at camp, though. Some girls were as old as 13. Lots of them knew tricks and soccer terms I'd never seen or heard before. I heard Lisa, the tall girl who had scored so many times, tell another girl that she'd been playing soccer since she was five and she'd already been to two soccer camps.

When Mom saw me icing my ankle, she must have noticed the frown on my face.

"Carmen, honey, what's wrong?" she asked.

Body language can tell you a lot about how a character feels.

Facial expressions can tell you how a character feels, too.

How do you think Carmen feels after her first day of soccer camp? Use details from the story to support your answer.

Aliyah's Answer:

Aliyah wrote a good answer to this question. Read what she wrote. Then answer the questions that follow. They will help you understand how Aliyah wrote her answer.

I think that after her first day Carmen is feeling really bad about herself. She keeps saying that she is not as good as the other girls who are playing. Carmen says that she feels confident when she is playing at home, but she seems nervous when she plays with the new girls. You can tell she is disappointed with herself when she hangs her head as she leaves the field. She is frowning when she puts ice on her ankle. Carmen had a really bad day, and she feels upset and frustrated because she doesn't think she played well.

What Makes Aliyah's Answer Work?

Aliyah wrote a successful answer because she carefully read the selection and answered the question. In addition, she also:

✓ noticed the way the author described Carmen's words and actions;

✓ used her observations to conclude that Carmen is disappointed, upset, and angry;

✓ included important details from the story;

✓ wrote in clear, complete sentences.

HINT!

Keep this checklist in mind when you write your answer:

✳ Did I state my main idea clearly?

✳ Have I answered the question completely?

✳ Have I used details from the story in my answer?

✳ Have I written sentences that are complete and interesting?

Let's take a closer look to see why Aliyah's answer would get a good score:

1. Aliyah clearly states her main idea.

In which sentence did she write her main idea? Write the sentence here.

_____

_____

_____

2. Aliyah provides details from the story that support her main idea. One detail is that Carmen keeps saying that she is not as good as the other girls.

Find another detail from the story that Aliyah includes to support her main idea. Write the sentence here.

_____

_____

_____

3. Aliyah also connects the ideas in her sentences. Here is one example:

Carmen says that she feels confident when she is playing at home, but she seems nervous when she plays with the new girls.

Find another sentence in which Aliyah connects two or more ideas. Write Aliyah's sentence here.

_____

_____

_____

4. Aliyah concludes her answer by making a general statement that sums up what she has already said about Carmen.

How does Aliyah sum up her answer? Write Aliyah's concluding sentence here.

_____

_____

_____

Tools & Tips

When you are writing about two or more ideas that are connected, it helps to use words or phrases that connect your ideas. Some words or phrases include:

but   and   which   yet

because   although   even though

Lamont wrote the following:

My friend Mark likes basketball. The players can do awesome tricks.

He could have written:

*My friend Mark likes basketball, **because** the players can do awesome tricks.*

Ashley wrote the following:

*My favorite book is **Matilda**. It is full of really fun characters.*

She could have written:

*My favorite book is **Matilda**, **which** is full of really fun characters.*

Sandy wrote the following:

My favorite drink is orange soda. It stains my teeth orange.

Connect Sandy's sentences using a connecting word or phrase.

_____

_____

_____

Lesson 5

Revising and Improving a Weak Answer

Here is another part of the story. It is followed by another question about the characters.

Carmen's Coach

I told my mom how bad my day had been. "I think I should switch to the intermediate group. It would be easier for me."

"I'm surprised," she said. "I thought you would like the challenge of the advanced group. You should talk to the head coach."

The next day my mom dropped me off early, and I found Tamara, the head coach. I tapped her on the shoulder. "Can I talk to you?"

"Sure," she said. "You're Carmen, right?"

Tamara knows Carmen's name. What does this tell you about Tamara?

I told her how I'd signed up for the advanced group, but that I didn't think I was good enough. "I can't keep up in the drills, and I let three people score goals. I want to switch down to the easier group."

Pay attention to Tamara's words and actions.

She didn't speak for a long moment, only looked at me seriously. Then she said, "Well, I saw you make some great passes. I thought you were giving Lisa a hard time out there. You look good enough for the advanced group to me."

"I don't think I am," I said quietly, my eyes on the ground.

"Look at me, Carmen," said Tamara. "You are a good player." She smiled. "You just need more confidence. You have to believe in your talents. I'll let you switch groups, but if you decide it's not challenging enough, let me know."

I found the intermediate group practicing on the far end of the field. The girls were doing dribbling drills, and I joined in. I realized quickly that today was different. I was taller and faster than many of the girls. I even scored a goal in the game that afternoon, even though I'm a midfielder and it's usually the forwards who score.

Do you think Tamara is a good coach? Use details from the story to support your answer.

Steven's Answer

Steven answered the question, but his answer needs improving:

> Tamara listens. She is very nice. And she lets Carmen do what she wants.

Improving Steven's Answer

Steven has answered part of the question. He has named three things about Tamara: She is a good listener; she is nice; she lets Carmen do what she wants. But Steven does not say if Tamara is a good coach, and he does not include details from the story to support his answer. In addition, he doesn't always write in complete sentences.

How could Steven improve his answer? The questions that follow help you revise and improve Steven's answer.

1. Steven hasn't stated his main idea clearly.

   Rewrite Steven's opening sentence so that it clearly expresses his main idea.

   _____

   _____

   _____

2. Steven says that Tamara is a good listener, but he doesn't given any details to support this statement.

   What could Steven add to show that Tamara is a good listener? What details can you find in the text? Rewrite this part of Steven's answer.

   _____

   _____

   _____

3. Steven says that Tamara is nice, but he doesn't give any details to support this statement.

   What details from the story could Steven add to show that Tamara is nice? Rewrite this part of Steven's answer.

   _____

   _____

   _____

4. Steven doesn't end his answer with a general statement that sums up the main idea.

   Write a new concluding sentence for Steven.

   _____

   _____

   _____

5. **Rewrite Steven's entire answer on the lines below.**

   _____

   _____

   _____

   _____

   _____

   _____

   _____

   _____

   _____

   _____

   _____

   _____

HINT!

Make sure your answer meets all the **SLAMS** tests.

SCORE BUILDER

Has your teacher ever responded to your writing with messages like the ones below?

Tell me more!   How do you know this?

Give more details!   Expand!

When you answer a question, your job is to provide enough details so people not familiar with the story understand the main idea. For example, imagine you traded papers with a partner, and you read the answer to this question: "What was bothering Sarah?"

Sarah was unhappy. This was going to be just like yesterday. No matter how hard she tried, she just didn't get it. She thought about the problem a long time. Then it came to her. She knew just what to do!

Ask yourself, "What did I learn from this answer?" Write your response here.

_____

_____

_____

Now ask yourself, "What *didn't* I learn from this answer? What do I still want to know?" Write your response here.

_____

_____

_____

Knowing the big ideas—for example, Sarah had a problem—is not enough. You have to provide details so that everyone who reads your answer can understand what is going on.

Lesson 6

Responding on Your Own

Here is the last part of the story. The question that follows on the next page is about understanding character.

Carmen Moves Up

Look for a clue here that shows how Carmen's feelings might change.

It was my third day at soccer camp, and I was sitting at the lunch table, eating a peanut-butter-and-jelly sandwich. I was thinking about the drills we'd done that morning. They were easy, maybe too easy.

Lisa, the great player from the advanced group, sat down next to me. "Weren't you in the advanced group on the first day? What happened?" she asked.

"Oh, well, I decided to move to intermediate. It seemed like everyone in the advanced group was way better than me."

"That's not true. I thought you were pretty hard to get by."

"Really? But you totally scored on us," I said.

"I saw you make a lot of great passes, and you're really fast."

I didn't know what to say. "Thanks," I mumbled.

After lunch, I talked to Tamara, the head coach. "It was really nice of you to let me switch down," I began, "and I've had a great time in the intermediate group."

"Let me guess," she said. "You want to switch back to advanced?"

"Well, I think I'm good enough to play in the advanced group, and I like the challenge."

She smiled. "They're playing a game in five minutes!"

What do Carmen's thoughts tell you about how she has changed?

I strapped on my shin guards and my cleats and ran out to join the group. Lisa gave me a high five, and the coach told me to start in the left midfield position. As the whistle blew and the game started, I felt a huge rush of excitement in my chest. I knew I'd be sore and stiff and that I'd fall down, but hopefully I'd learn too. Whatever happened, I knew I could do it.

Do you think Carmen has changed? Use details from the story to support your answer.

Write your answer on the lines below.

_____

_____

_____

_____

_____

_____

_____

_____

_____

_____

_____

_____

_____

_____

_____

_____

_____

_____

_____

HINT!

When you have finished, check your answer:

* Have you identified how Carmen has changed?

* Have you supported your ideas with details from the story?

* Does your answer meet all of the SLAMS tests?

Reader's Response!
Revise & Edit

When you have finished writing, exchange papers with a partner. As you read each other's work, answer the questions that follow.

1 Did the writer state the main idea clearly?   ___Yes ___ No
If not, what needs to be added or changed?
Write your response here.

_____

_____

2 Did the writer explain how Carmen changed?   ___ Yes ___ No
If not, what needs to be added or fixed?
Write your response here.

_____

_____

3 Did the writer support his or her ideas
with details from the story?   ___ Yes ___ No
If not, what needs to be added or changed?
Write your response here.

_____

_____

_____

4 Has the writer followed all the SLAMS rules?   ___ **Yes** ___ **No**
If not, which rules were not followed?
Check all the boxes that apply.

S ___   L ___   A ___   M ___   S ___

5 **Give the paper back to your partner to revise and edit.**

Reviewing the Question

Questions about understanding characters usually focus on three elements:

- What is the character like? How do you know this?

- How does the character change? How do you know this?

- Why does the character behave or act the way he or she does? How do you know this?

Notice that each question has two parts.

- The first part asks you to describe the character.

- The second part asks you to find details from the text to support your description.

Questions about understanding character may also ask you to compare or contrast two characters. For example:

At the beginning of the story, Jolene says, "You are my best friend ever, Miranda. Sometimes I think we could be twins." In what ways do you think Jolene and Miranda are alike? Use details from the story to support your answer.

When answering questions about character, be sure to include details about what the character does, what the character says, and the character's facial expressions and body language. All these details are clues to understanding character.

Fact & Opinion

How often have you had a conversation like this one?

Boy: I have Ms. Chanin this year. She's really great!

Girl: Lucky you. I have Mr. Ryan. He's so strict. He gave us 20 math problems for homework over the weekend, and they were really hard.

Boy: That's a lot. We had only 10 problems, and Ms. Chanin explained how to do them in class. She's the best teacher I have ever had.

This conversation demonstrates two types of information.

- We state **facts**. "I have Ms. Chanin this year" is a fact.

- We express **opinions**. "She's really great!" is an opinion.

What's the difference?

A statement of fact can be checked. You can look up the information and find out whether it's true or false.

An opinion cannot be checked. It's an expression of the speaker's personal feelings. You can back up an opinion—provide evidence to support it—but you can't prove that an opinion is true or false.

Lesson 7

What Makes a Good Answer?

This selection includes both opinions and facts.

Does Organic Food Make a Difference?

What does it mean when the United States Department of Agriculture puts its "organic" label on an egg or a plum or a bag of flour? It means that the food has been raised or grown without chemical pesticides. No antibiotics or growth hormones have been used either. These foods usually cost more than foods without the "organic" label because they are more expensive for the farmer to produce. But are they healthier to eat?

This paragraph is loaded with facts.

The Department of Agriculture doesn't claim that the "organic" label means the food is better for you. The label just tells you that the food has been produced in a special way. For example, all the wheat, rice, and corn in a 100% organic cereal was grown without chemicals. By law, farmers can't use chemicals for at least three years before their wheat, rice, and corn can be called "organic."

Without chemical pesticides, organic food is probably safer for you. However, the organic label doesn't say that the food is more nutritious. Even so, many people believe that organic food contains more nutrients because of the way it's grown. They are happy to spend more money on organic foods if it means being healthier.

Doctors and experts in nutrition have their own views on organic foods. "The important thing is to eat a reasonable, balanced diet," says Dr. Stephen Long. "You don't need to spend the extra money on fruits, breads, and meats that are labeled 'organic.'"

The words in quotes share opinions.

"I agree," says nutritionist Dr. Rachel Fuller. "Stop worrying if that apple you're eating was treated with chemical pesticides. It's more important to worry about cholesterol. Learn to read the labels and stay away from the foods that are bad for you."

Other doctors and nutritionists urge us to take an additional step. They encourage us to look for the label that tells us the food is organic.

What have you learned about organic foods? Use facts from the selection in your answer.

Tran's Answer:

Tran wrote a good answer to this question.

This selection told me that there are different opinions about organic food. Some people believe that organic food is more nutritious. Other people believe that organic food isn't really better than other foods. I learned that the organic label only means one thing. It means that the food is grown a certain way. The farmers can't use chemicals or antibiotics or growth hormones. The organic label doesn't mean that the food has more vitamins.

I've also learned that organic food costs more. That's because it is more expensive for farmers to produce. As a result, the prices for organic foods are higher.

HINT!

Test scorers look for the following things:

* A clear statement of the main idea.

* A clear understanding of the difference between facts and opinions.

* Facts from the selection to develop the main idea.

* Complete, correct, and interesting sentences.

What Makes Tran's Answer Work?

Let's analyze Tran's answer by answering the questions on the next page.

1. Tran starts with a sentence that states the main idea. The sentence also states the first thing that Tran learned from the reading selection.

   What is Tran's opening sentence? Write it here. Circle the words that state the main idea.

   _____

   _____

   _____

2. Tran shows clearly that he understands the difference between facts and opinions. Here is one fact he includes in the first paragraph: "I learned that the organic label only means one thing."

   Find another fact that Tran includes in the first paragraph. Write it here.

   _____

   _____

   _____

3. Tran's first paragraph is about what the organic label means. All the facts in the paragraph develop that idea.

   What is Tran's second paragraph about? Write the main idea of the second paragraph here.

   _____

   _____

   _____

4. Tran includes a fact from the selection to support his idea in the second paragraph.

   What fact does he include? Write a fact from the second paragraph here.

   _____

   _____

Tools & Tips

A **fact** is something that you can check. For example:

✓ Someone tells you it's raining outside. You can step out the door to check.

✓ Someone tells you the cake is chocolate. You can find out by tasting it.

✓ Someone tells you the movie begins at 2:15. You can phone the movie theater or look in the newspaper to make sure.

An **opinion** is something that you cannot check. For example:

✓ Someone tells you that rainy days are better than sunny days. You may agree or disagree, but you can't step out the door and check whether this is true.

✓ Someone tells you that the chocolate cake is the best she has ever eaten. You can taste the cake and either agree or disagree, but you can't prove her statement is true.

✓ Someone tells you that 2:15 is not a good time to go to the movies. You may share these feelings or not, but you can't call the movie theater or look in the newspaper to find out whether this statement is true.

Read the sentences below. Write **F** next to each sentence that states a **fact**. Write an **O** next to each sentence that states an **opinion**.

_____ **1.** Your plan for raising money is too complicated.

_____ **2.** At Olive Street School, the bake sale brought in $175.

_____ **3.** Selling wrapping paper is easier than selling houseplants.

_____ **4.** People seem to like wrapping paper better.

_____ **5.** You have to water houseplants if you don't want them to die.

Lesson 8

Revising and Improving a Weak Answer

This reading selection contains both facts and opinions. The question that follows asks you to identify both.

What Do You Think?

"Did you read that article we had for homework?" Andrew asked.

"Yes," Lydia answered. "I thought it was very interesting. You know, my mother won't buy food that isn't organic. She says that food without the organic labels might be full of pesticides and other poisons."

"That's what my dad says!" Ryan joined in. "Eating food that's organic is better for you, even though it costs more."

"That's right," Lydia agreed. "When fruits and vegetables are treated with pesticides, farmers get rid of insects and molds that might destroy the plants, but they also might destroy important vitamins."

"I think it's gross that they put poison on the food we eat," exclaimed Andrew.

"On the other hand," said Ryan, "if the farmers didn't use pesticides, maybe our food would be even more gross. Maybe there would be worms in everything, and big holes where caterpillars had eaten our lettuce and spinach."

"Well," said Lydia, "I happen to think organic food tastes better. Last summer, we had some cherries from an organic farm. They were the best I've ever eaten. Everyone in my family said so."

"But it is expensive," Andrew pointed out. "If you can't afford to buy organic food, does that mean you have to eat food that's not as good for you?"

"You guys have some interesting ideas," said Ms. Graff, their teacher. "Why don't you come in, get seated, and give us all a chance to hear what you have to say."

What is Andrew's opinion of pesticides?

What does Lydia think about how organic foods taste?

What opinions about organic foods do the students in this selection express? Use details from the selection in your answer.

Dominique's Answer:

Dominique wrote an answer to this question, but it is incomplete.

> The students in this selection say lots of different stuff. Like that eating organic food is better for you. They say that it tastes better. They say that all farmers should stop using chemicals.

Improving Dominique's Answer

Dominique gives a few of the opinions expressed in the selection, but her response would not get a good score because she doesn't answer the question completely. Her first sentence is very vague; it doesn't state clearly what her main idea is. Her second sentence needs work, too; it's not a complete sentence. To improve her answer, she needs a clearer statement of her main idea. She also needs to include more details from the selection and to write more correct sentences.

Use the questions that follow to help you improve Dominique's answer.

1. Dominique needs to state her main idea more clearly.

   Rewrite her opening sentence to make the main idea clearer. Write the new sentence here.

Test scorers look for the following things:

* A clear statement of the main idea.

* A clear understanding of the difference between facts and opinions.

* Opinions from the selection to develop the main idea.

* Complete, correct and interesting sentences.

_____

_____

_____

_____

2. Dominique's second sentence is not complete. Sentences like this are called fragments.

   Rewrite Dominique's second sentence to correct the fragment.

   _____

   _____

   _____

3. Dominique's second and third sentences contain opinions about organic food being better than regular food.

   Find two more opinions in the reading selection that are about the same topic. Write two new sentences that could follow Dominique's third sentence.

   _____

   _____

   _____

   _____

   _____

4. Dominique's last sentence is on a different topic—the use of chemicals.

   Find two more opinions in the reading selection that are about chemicals. Write two new sentences that could be inserted before Dominique's last sentence.

   _____

   _____

   _____

   _____

   _____

   _____

HINT!

The sentences for #4 could be a separate paragraph.

SCORE BUILDER

If you're not sure whether someone is expressing an opinion, here are some clues to look for.

✓ An opinion often contains words like **I think, I feel, I believe,** and **in my opinion.**

> *I believe chocolate is very good for you.*

> *It's too late, I think, to watch television tonight.*

✓ An opinion often contains words like **most, best, greatest,** and **worst.**

> *This is the greatest book I've ever read.*

> *That is the worst song I've ever heard.*

✓ An opinion sometimes contains words like **might, could,** and **would.**

> *An apple might taste very good right now.*

> *If the label says "organic," it could mean that the food has more vitamins in it.*

Write three opinions of your own on the lines below. Use some of the clue words in your sentences.

1 _____

_____

2 _____

_____

3 _____

_____

58

Lesson 9

Responding on Your Own

The final reading selection is an editorial written by Ms. Graff's students and sent to a local newspaper. The question that follows asks you to express and explain your own opinions.

Taking Care of Ourselves and the World

This semester in our health class, we have been learning about nutrition. We have found out something very interesting. The word "organic" means that food is grown without chemical pesticides or fertilizers. Many people, therefore, believe that organic food is better for their health than non-organic food. How do we know? Even though it is more expensive, people are buying more organic foods than ever.

Between 2002 and 2003, the sale of organic foods went way up. There was an increase of 77.8% in the sale of organic meat and fish. The sale of organic breads and cereals went up almost 23%. The increase in the sale of organic snacks was more than 29%.

The organic snack foods, like chips and cookies, are especially interesting. Some of these snacks are made by the same companies that make non-organic chips and cookies. The organic label doesn't mean that these snacks are healthier. Many of them still have salt, fat, and sweeteners. People see words like "natural" and "organic," and they think these snacks are good for them. So they end up eating organic chips instead of apples or carrots.

Along with the health benefits, people also buy organic foods because they may be better for the environment. Organic farmers use methods that don't harm the soil. They don't waste resources either. Many of them recycle the parts of the plants that they don't use into compost to enrich the soil. That makes organic food not only good for us but good for the planet, too.

> *Look for facts to support your opinion.*

> *Look for more facts here to support your answer.*

What is your opinion? Do you think organic food is worth the extra cost? Why or why not? Use facts from all three reading selections in this unit and your own experience and ideas to support your opinion.

Write your answer on the lines below.

_____

_____

_____

_____

_____

_____

_____

_____

_____

_____

_____

_____

_____

_____

_____

_____

_____

HINT!

When you are finished, check your answer.

✳ Is your opinion clearly stated?

✳ Have you used facts, not other opinions, to support your position?

✳ Does your answer meet all the SLAMS tests?

Reader's Response!
Revise & Edit

When you have finished writing, exchange papers with a partner. As you read each other's work, answer the questions below.

1 Did the writer fully answer the question?   ___ Yes ___ No
If not, what needs to be added or changed?

Write your response here.

_____

_____

_____

2 Did the writer use facts from the selections?   ___ Yes ___ No
If not, what needs to be added or changed?

Write your response here.

_____

_____

_____

3 Was the answer clear and easy to understand?   ___ Yes ___ No
If not, what needs to be added or changed?

Write your response here.

_____

_____

_____

4 Has the writer followed all the SLAMS rules?   ___ Yes ___ No
If not, which rules were not followed?

Check all the boxes that apply.

S ___   L ___   A ___   M ___   S ___

5 **Give the paper back to your partner to revise and edit.**

Reviewing the Question

Make sure that you know the difference between fact and opinion.

- Remember that a **fact** can be checked in some way. You can look it up or see for yourself whether it's true or not.

- An **opinion** expresses someone's feelings or beliefs. You can't prove an opinion to be true or false, right or wrong.

You will find both facts and opinions in many reading selections, and you will include both facts and opinions in your own writing.

Just remember that when you express an opinion, you need to make it convincing and believable. The only way to do that is to back up your opinion with facts.

Read this selection. Then answer the questions that follow.

And the Winner Is...

Everyone was talking about it. For the first time ever, Maple Avenue School was giving a prize to the student who best represented the school's values.

"What does that mean—'values'?" asked Jason. "Is it the most honest person or the one with the most courage?"

"I just think it's the one that makes the least amount of trouble," said Ali. "You know, the one the teachers like the best because he or she doesn't mess around in class."

"Wait a minute," interrupted Selena. "There's a list here that tells what the school is looking for." She pointed to a notice hanging on the bulletin board in the hall.

THE SCHOOL BOARD IS AWARDING A PRIZE OF $250...

To the 5th-grade student who has the qualities and values we want Maple Avenue students to develop!

- Must be a good student.
- Must be a good citizen of the school and the community.
- Must be well-rounded.
- Must show leadership.

We encourage teachers and students to make recommendations.

"That sounds hard to judge," said Jason. "I mean, you can figure out who's a good student by looking at the person's grades, but how do you know what makes someone a good citizen?"

"It sounds like one opinion versus another," Ali agreed.

"I don't think so," said Selena. "If I say you're a good citizen of the school, that's my opinion, but I have to back it up with facts. For instance, Jason, you help with the school recycling project. You're a playground monitor for the younger kids, too. And you always hold the door open for a teacher who is carrying a lot of books and stuff."

"Well, maybe," Jason said slowly.

Ali still insisted that it was just an opinion. "Jason can say that you show leadership, Selena, but I might think you're just bossy."

"Leadership is a hard one," Jason said, "but 'well-rounded' might be a better example. If I say Selena is well-rounded, it's because she's good at a lot of things. She gets good grades, she draws great cartoons, she plays the drums, and she's on the soccer team."

Selena nodded her head in agreement, but Ali wasn't convinced. "Sounds like you've made up your mind—this prize is Selena's," she grumbled

"C'mon, Ali" Selena coaxed. "Any one of us could win. Look at you! You're a better soccer player than I am, and a better drummer. Maybe you're not good at art, but you write great poems. You even won a prize for your poetry."

"I still don't think I could win," she replied. "Think about the leadership thing. When Jason gets an idea, he can talk anyone into helping him. That's how he got the school recycling project going."

"Stop putting yourself down," Jason scolded. "I think Selena's right. I think we all have a chance. Let's go to the office and recommend each other for this prize."

1 Main Idea and Supporting Details

Summarize this story. What is it mostly about? Use details from the selection in your summary.

_____

_____

_____

_____

_____

_____

_____

_____

_____

_____

_____

_____

_____

_____

_____

_____

_____

_____

_____

_____

_____

_____

2 Understanding Characters

How does Ali change by the end of the story? Support your answer with details from the story.

_____

_____

_____

_____

_____

_____

_____

_____

_____

_____

_____

_____

_____

_____

_____

_____

_____

_____

_____

_____

3 Fact and Opinion

Who do you think the judges will choose to win the Maple Avenue School prize? What facts will they use to back up their choice? Use details from the story and your own ideas to answer this question.

_____

_____

_____

_____

_____

_____

_____

_____

_____

_____

_____

_____

_____

_____

_____

_____

_____

_____

_____

_____

Part B

Writing Extended Answers

Reading What Is on the Page

You have practiced identifying main ideas and supporting details. "Reading what is on the page" is very much like finding main ideas and supporting details. You are reading to discover the facts and information in a selection.

Many open-ended questions ask you to do just this. You don't need to draw conclusions about what you have read. You don't need to connect the selection to your own experience. You just need to understand the information as it is written.

In this unit, you will read a nonfiction selection about inventions. The questions that follow test your understanding of what is "on the page."

70

Lesson 10

What Makes a Good Answer?

Read this nonfiction selection about inventions.

Accidental Inventions

Have you ever taken a long walk in the woods or in a park? Have you ever played in long grass or weeds? If so, you may have come home covered with burrs. Burrs are prickly seed pods that stick to your socks and clothing. They are a bother to remove, and they must be pulled off one by one. If they get tangled in a dog's fur, they may need to be cut out carefully with scissors. Burrs aren't painful or dangerous, they're just pesky little things.

Now, can you use this information to invent something?

George de Mestral could and did. He was a Swiss engineer who returned from a walk one day to find himself and his dog covered with burrs. He was curious to find out just why they stuck so well to fur and clothing. So he put a burr under a microscope and soon had his answer. Each prickle on the burr ended in a tiny hook. The hooks on the burrs got caught in the tangles of fur and cloth fibers, and consequently the burrs stuck to Mr. de Mestral's clothing and his dog.

That's when de Mestral got his great idea. What a wonderful way to stick two pieces of material together! If he could do it just right, the two pieces would stick together like burrs to a dog, but you could peel the pieces apart when you wanted to separate them.

It took almost ten years before de Mestral and the people who worked with him were able to perfect a system of tiny hooks and loops that worked like burrs and fur, but they succeeded. We know the final product today as Velcro®.

> The story of Velcro is a supporting detail.

Chance or luck plays a big part in many inventions. An inventor accidentally makes—or stumbles onto—something useful that he or she wasn't trying to make or find at all. This kind of luck has a special name. It's called serendipity (pronounced SEH-ren-DIP-it-ee). It was sheer serendipity that led to the invention of Velcro.

The main idea is expressed in this paragraph.

For another example of serendipity, take one invention made at the 3M Company. 3M makes many things, but it's best known for its sticky tape. If you've ever used Scotch® brand tape, you've used a 3M product.

As you can imagine, the people at 3M are always trying to make newer and better glues. One scientist, Dr. Spencer Silver, was working with a formula he hoped would make a great glue. The glue turned out to be terrible. It could hardly stick two pieces of paper together. Dr. Silver sadly put it aside.

Another 3M employee named Art Fry turned Dr. Silver's useless glue into a useful invention. On Sundays, Mr. Fry sang in his church choir. He needed a way to mark the pages of his hymn book so that he could quickly find the hymns he was supposed to sing. The little pieces of paper he used always fell out of the book.

Then he thought of Dr. Silver's "useless" glue. The next day at work, he coated the ends of some small pieces of paper with the glue. They stuck to the pages of the hymn book, but they easily came off without damaging the pages. They worked perfectly, and the Post-it® note was born.

The story of the Post-it is a supporting detail.

Today, sticky little Post-it notes are everywhere. You can find Post-it messages on refrigerators, on doors, next to telephones, even on TV screens. People stick short messages on their office documents, books, and file folders.

Silver and Fry were the inventors, but serendipity also deserves some of the credit. However, luck alone can't make an invention. You also need someone smart enough to see the new possibilities in something seemingly useless, like an outdoor burr or non-stick glue.

The main idea is restated here.

As one scientist said, "Chance favors the prepared mind."

Read the instructions below. Notice that they don't ask you to write a paragraph. Instead they ask you to complete a chart.

The chart below compares the invention of Velcro to the invention of the Post-it. Read the chart carefully. Complete the chart with additional facts from the selection.

Here is how Camilla completed the chart. Read what she wrote. Then answer the questions that follow to see what makes Camilla's answers successful.

Camilla's Answers:

Comparing Velcro and Post-its

Velcro	Post-it
sticks two pieces of cloth together	sticks two pieces of paper together
uses hooks and loops to stick	uses glue to stick
you can pull the two pieces of cloth apart easily	you can pull the two pieces of paper apart easily
idea came from burrs in a dog's fur	idea came from paper used to mark hymn book and from weak glue
invented by a Swiss engineer	invented by someone at the 3M company

What Makes Camilla's Answer Work?

Camilla does exactly what the test scorers look for:

✓ She reads the selection and the question very carefully.

✓ She pays attention to the information the question asks for.

✓ She knows where to find each piece of information in the reading selection.

✓ She answers the question exactly by giving all the information that is needed, but nothing extra.

Now let's take a closer look at Camilla's answer to see what makes it successful.

1. In order to fill in the first blank, Camilla looked at the first piece of information in the chart about the Post-it. That way she could figure out what kind of information she needed about Velcro.

   What kind of information about both inventions is in the first part of the chart? Write your answer here.

   _____

   _____

   _____

2. For the second blank, Camilla figured out which information to fill in by reading the information in the chart about Velcro.

   What information about both inventions is in the second part of the chart? Write your answer here.

   _____

   _____

   _____

3. Look at the fourth part of the chart.

   What kind of information did Camilla need for this part? Write your answer here.

   _____

   _____

   _____

4. To fill in the last part, Camilla needed to find information about who invented the Post-it.

   Where in the selection did she find this information? Write your answer here.

   _____

   _____

   _____

Tools & Tips

The title of a chart contains important information. For example, the title of the chart on page 72 tells the purpose of the chart. Turn back to page 72 and look at the title.

1. What is the purpose of this chart?

_____

_____

A chart is usually read in two directions—across and down. The chart on page 72 has two columns, or lists. Each column has a heading. The heading tells you about the information in each column.

2. Which information appears in the first column?

_____

_____

3. Which information appears in the second column?

_____

_____

4. Now try reading across—from left to right—instead of down. What do you learn when you read the first item in the first column, and then the first item in the second column?

_____

_____

_____

Strategy: Find Information in the Selection

Camilla's answer was successful because she knew how to find information in the reading selection. In order to complete the chart, she needed information about how the Post-it sticks. What did she do?

✓ First, she looked for the word *Post-it* in the reading selection.

✓ Then she looked for the word *stick* and related words like *stuck* and *sticky*. That took her to the story of Dr. Silver's useless glue.

What words helped Camilla find information about the purpose of Velcro?

_____

_____

Words that help you find information are called **keywords**. Keywords open up the reading selection to show you the information you need.

Try finding keywords. Read these paragraphs. Then identify the keywords that help you answer the questions.

1. Some inventions are accidental, and some are purposeful—the result of long, hard work. The invention of the ballpoint pen is a good example of a purposeful invention. It was invented more than once. The first attempt was in 1888 in the United States. Then it was invented again in Hungary in 1935, and once more in the United States after World War Two. Each time, the inventors were trying to do the same thing. At that time pens that wrote with ink had to be refilled frequently. So all of the inventors of the ballpoint pen looked for a way to write with ink without having to stop to refill the pen.

a. What invention is being described?

_____

_____

_____

What keywords helped you find the answer?

_____

b. What were the inventors trying to do?

_____

_____

_____

What keywords helped you find the answer?

_____

2. The ballpoint pen was an improvement on the fountain pen in two ways. First of all, the ballpoint pen wrote with a roller ball instead of a sharp, pointy tip. It also had a big supply of its own ink. The roller ball wasn't hard to make, but the ink was a huge problem. It had to be thin enough to flow evenly, but it couldn't be too thin or the pen would leak. On the other hand, if the ink was too thick, it wouldn't flow at all. The pen would get clogged and refuse to write, or it would suddenly produce a big, sticky ink glob that smeared all over. It took more than 60 years and many different attempts to solve this problem.

a. How is the ballpoint pen better than the fountain pen?

_____

_____

_____

What keywords helped you find the answer?

_____

b. What was the most difficult part of this invention?

_____

_____

_____

What keywords helped you find the answer?

_____

Strategy: Organize Your Answer

When answers to open-ended questions are extended, it is important to organize them clearly. A well-organized answer makes it easier for readers to understand what you are writing.

However, when you need to compare and contrast two things, the way Camilla did in this unit, organization can sometimes be tricky. When you are comparing, you are noting similarities—things that are alike. When you are contrasting, you are noting differences—things that are not alike.

What's the easiest way to do both in one answer?

Many people organize ideas in a *graphic organizer* called a **Venn diagram**. A Venn diagram shows both *similarities* and *differences*. Suppose that you are comparing and contrasting two things called **A** and **B**. Here is how the comparison and contrast would look on a Venn Diagram:

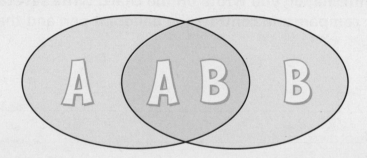

1. Which parts of the Venn diagram show the differences between A and B?

_____

_____

2. Which part of the Venn diagram shows the similarities between A and B?

_____

_____

The Venn diagram lets you see the differences and the similarities very clearly. You can then organize your information using this diagram.

Try this strategy with the information about ballpoint pens and fountain pens in Lesson 11 (pages 75–76). Be sure to write a heading for each part of the circles.

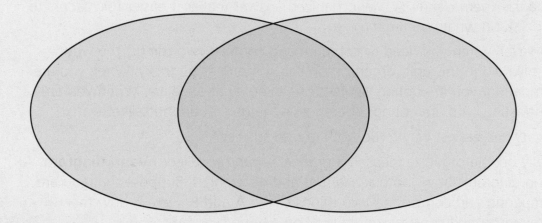

Now use the information you wrote on the chart. Write several sentences that compare and contrast the ballpoint pen and the fountain pen.

_____

_____

_____

_____

_____

_____

_____

_____

_____

Revising and Improving a Weak Answer

You have seen what a good answer looks like. Your analysis of a good answer has also given you some tools you can use to revise an answer that is not as good. Here is another question about the reading selection *Accidental Inventions*. Read the question carefully; then look at the answer that follows.

> **How are the two inventions in this selection—Velcro and Post-its—alike? How are they different? Use details from the selection to support your answer.**

Malcolm's Answer:

Malcolm tried to answer the question above. Read his answer carefully. Then use the questions that follow to help you revise and improve his answer.

> They're alike because they stick stuff together. And you can pull the stuff apart. But they make different kinds of things stick. Their inventors were different, too.

Improving Malcolm's Answer

Malcolm wrote part of an answer:

✓ He named two similarities.

✓ He also named two differences.

Malcolm has the basic idea of comparing and contrasting. However, his answer is not complete. He needs to include more details about both the similarities and the differences. He also needs to write an opening and a closing sentence.

Imagine that you wrote Malcolm's answer. Ask yourself the questions on the following pages to help you revise and improve it.

1. Have I included an opening that states what I am comparing and contrasting?

   If not, what sentence or sentences can I add at the beginning of my answer? Write the opening sentence here.

   _____

   _____

   _____

   _____

2. Have I said enough about the two similarities I name?

   If not, what details can I add to make my answer more complete? Write the new sentences here.

   _____

   _____

   _____

   _____

   _____

3. Have I included enough similarities in my answer?

   If not, what similarities can I add to make my answer more complete? Write the new sentences here.

   _____

   _____

   _____

   _____

4. Have I said enough about the two differences I name?

   If not, what details can I add to make my answer more complete?

   _____

   _____

   _____

   _____

5. Have I included enough differences in my answer?

If not, what differences can I add to make my answer more complete? Write the new sentences here.

_____

_____

_____

_____

_____

6. Do I have a good closing sentence?

If not, what can I add at the end of my answer? Write the closing here.

_____

_____

_____

_____

_____

SCORE BUILDER

When you write an answer that compares and contrasts, pay special attention to your choice of words. You need to let your readers know when you are mentioning similarities and when you are mentioning differences.

Here are some ways to signal your readers that you are discussing **similarities**:

✓ Whales and elephants are **both** mammals.

✓ The whale, **like** the elephant, is a mammal.

✓ Whales and elephants are **similar** because they are mammals.

1. Write a sentence that compares whales and elephants by stating that both are large. Use a signal word in your sentence.

_____

_____

Here are some ways to signal your readers that you are discussing **differences**:

✓ Whales live in the ocean, **but** elephants live on land.

✓ Whales live in the ocean; elephants, **however**, live on land.

✓ Whales live in the ocean. Elephants, **on the other hand**, live on land.

2. Write a sentence that contrasts whales and elephants by stating that elephants eat vegetation but whales eat fish. Use a signal word in your sentence.

_____

_____

Responding on Your Own

Here is another question about the reading selection *Accidental Inventions*. This time you will answer on your own, without models or questions to help you. As you plan and write your answer, think about what you have learned from studying Camilla's answer and improving Malcolm's answer. You should also use the following things to help you write your answer:

✓ the **strategies** you have practiced

✓ the tips you were given in **Tools & Tips**

✓ the reminders in the **Score Builder**

Notice that this question, like the first two, asks you about what is on the page. Answer the question by using the details and examples from the reading selection.

> **In what ways are both Velcro and Post-its "accidental inventions"? Use details from the selection to support your answer.**

Write your answer on the lines below.

_____

_____

_____

_____

_____

_____

HINT!

The test scorers look for the following things:

✳ A clear statement of your main idea.

✳ A complete answer to the question.

✳ Relevant supporting details from the selection.

✳ Clear, complete, sentences.

Reader's Response!
Revise & Edit

When you have finished writing, exchange papers with a partner. As you read each other's answers, follow these steps:

1 Did the writer answer the question? ___ **Yes** ___ **No**
If not, what needs to be added?
Write your response here.

_____

_____

_____

2 Did the writer use enough, relevant details for support? ___ **Yes** ___ **No**
If not, what details need to be changed?
Write your response here.

_____

_____

_____

3 Did the writer organize the answer clearly? ___ **Yes** ___ **No**
If not, what needs to be changed?
Write your response here.

_____

_____

4 Has the writer followed all the SLAMS rules? ___ **Yes** ___ **No**
If not, which rules were not followed?
Check all the boxes that apply.

S ___   L ___   A ___   M ___   S ___

5 **Give the paper back to your partner to revise and edit.**

Reviewing the Question

Reading what is on the page is another way of saying **reading for information**. Here are some ways you might be asked a question about what is on the page. Pay special attention to the words in **dark** type.

- **How** does Velcro stick?

- **When** did 3M's useless glue finally get used?

- **What** are the differences between the fountain pen and the ballpoint pen?

- **What** did George de Mestral learn from brushing his dog?

- **Why** did Art Fry want sticky paper?

- **How** does the modern ballpoint pen work?

Notice that these questions all ask for information that can be found on the page. To answer them, you need to look for information in the selection that tells how or when or why or what.

Reading Between the Lines

In the last unit you wrote about what was "on the page." You also need to **make inferences** about what you are reading. That is, you have to be able to figure out information that is not directly stated on the page. This is called **reading between the lines**.

For example, look carefully at the following sentences.

- Carlos turned and ran up the stairs. The door to his room banged shut behind him.

- The death camas has a surprisingly pretty little flower.

- Chantelle tightened her seat belt nervously and looked out the window at the mountains below.

You can probably figure out that—

- Carlos is angry or upset.

- Judging from its name, it's not a good idea to eat the death camas.

- Chantelle is in an airplane or on a high mountain road in a car or bus.

The sentences don't actually say these things, but if you read between the lines, you can figure out what is happening. This is what it means to make inferences.

In this unit, you will write answers to open-ended questions that ask you to make inferences by reading between the lines.

Lesson 15

What Makes a Good Answer?

Read the story below. The question that follows asks when the story takes place.

If Walls Could Talk

How does the man light up the cave? What does this tell you?

What is special about these animals?

The dim, dancing light of the torch fire casts the shadow of a crouching man onto the cave wall. Old Aknatat the Spirit Hunter reaches deep into a crack in the wall and brings out a small skin bag. Before opening it, he lightly touches all the sacred animal drawings that cover the walls and ceiling of the cave, and he speaks a few words to each one. His people hunt these animals for food—the great wild ox, the shaggy wild horse, the giant deer, the huge mammoth. Old Aknatat himself and generations of Spirit Hunters before him made these drawings. Each drawing has its own history. Each one has brought his people luck in the hunt.

Old Aknatat is proud to be his people's Spirit Hunter, but it is a lonely occupation. Few people ever see the drawings of power. The Spirit Hunter must work alone.

He turns to one charcoal drawing low on the wall in front of him. He pauses, then takes a corner of the bearskin robe he is wearing and scrubs at the drawing until it is completely erased.

Soon, one of his students will come into the cave. This boy is different. Old Aknatat can feel it. The boy may be the first Chosen Child in a generation. If the boy passes the test, Aknatat will start teaching him the special secrets and mysteries that will make him the next Spirit Hunter.

Old Aknatat reaches into the bag, takes out a single stick of charcoal, and waits.

He hears the boy coming. It is the first time the boy has been allowed to come all the way into the cave, and in the blackness he stumbles over loose rocks.

Old Aknatat smiles. He used to stumble, too, many years past. But he has been coming into the cave for a long time now, and he knows the location of every stone. The boy does not cry out. This is good, for the cave is a sacred place. It would not do to show pain in front of the spirits.

Finally, the boy enters the enormous room where the old man is sitting. The hesitant torch flame lights up the cave walls, and the boy sees, for the first time, the sacred drawings all around him.

Wordlessly, the old man hands the charcoal to the boy and points at the newly blank spot on the cave wall. It is time for the boy to show what he can do.

The boy looks uncertain. "You—you want *me* to draw something?" he asks.

Old Aknatat makes the smallest of nods.

"What do you want me to draw?" the boy asks.

Aknatat looks at him for a long while. "The wall will tell you what to draw," he says finally.

"Walls cannot speak, Master," says the boy timidly.

Aknatat says nothing, simply gazes at the boy. Has he guessed wrong? Will this one fail, like so many others before him?

The boy hesitates. Then he touches the wall. Slowly, slowly, he feels the power of the drawings flowing into his fingers. He runs his hand along the wall. It is cold and damp and lumpy. His fingers feel around one of the lumps. And then—a picture slowly builds in his imagination. The wall is speaking to him. He sees a powerful, running figure, an immense animal with a stout body, short but thick legs, a thick neck, and powerful shoulders topped by a hump of muscle. The head is long and carried low. Two horns arch up from its nose. He sketches the animal on the wall, at first hesitantly, then with quick, confident strokes.

It is the Great Woolly Rhinoceros, the symbol of his people—the one animal his people do not hunt.

It is the drawing that Old Aknatat erased, the drawing that he drew many years before when he became a Spirit Hunter, the drawing that all Spirit Hunters before him drew.

The old man looks at the drawing of the Great Woolly Rhino and nods. His student understands what the wall is telling him. He is a Chosen One.

Old Aknatat picks up the torch, motions to the boy, and the two make their way back to the surface to begin the boy's training.

Do woolly rhinos exist today? What does this tell you?

When does this story take place? Use details from the story to explain your answer.

Jen's Answer:

Here is Jen's answer. Read what she wrote. Then answer the questions that follow to see what makes Jen's answer a good one.

This story takes place a long time ago. It probably takes place many thousands of years ago.

In the story, Old Aknatat is looking at drawings of animals on the walls of a cave. He drew some of them himself. Others were drawn by people before him. People don't do this today. They don't make animal drawings on the walls of caves. They only made them thousands of years ago, when people lived in caves and made drawings and paintings on cave walls.

A second thing that tells you the story takes place long ago is the kinds of animals in the drawings. There is a wild ox and a giant deer and a mammoth. The boy draws a woolly rhinoceros. All the animals in the drawings became extinct thousands of years ago. These kinds of animals don't exist any more.

A third thing that tells you that the story takes place long ago is that wild horses are among the drawings of animals that Aknatat's people hunt. People stopped hunting horses for food thousands of years ago. We ride horses today. We don't hunt them.

What Makes Jen's Answer Work?

Jen does all the things that the test scorers look for:

✓ She answers the question clearly in her opening sentences.

✓ She gives several reasons for her answer.

✓ She uses a lot of details from the story.

✓ She writes clear, complete, and interesting sentences.

Now let's take a closer look at Jen's answer to see why it is successful.

1. Jen answers the question in her opening paragraph.

   What is Jen's answer? Write her answer here.

   _____

   _____

   _____

2. In paragraph 2, Jen states the first reason for her answer.

   a. **What is Jen's first reason? Write her reason here.**

   _____

   _____

   _____

   b. **What supporting details does she include? Write your answer here.**

   _____

   _____

   _____

3. In paragraph 3, Jen gives her second reason.

   a. **What is Jen's second reason? Write her reason here.**

   _____

   _____

   _____

   b. **What supporting details does she include? Write your answer here.**

   _____

   _____

   _____

4. In the last paragraph, Jen gives her third reason.

   a. **What is Jen's third reason? Write her reason here.**

   _____

   _____

   _____

   b. **What supporting details does she include? Write your answer here.**

   _____

   _____

   _____

5. Jen's sentences are clear and interesting. They are also complete sentences that begin with a capital letter and end with a period. For example "In the story Old Aknatat is looking at drawings of animals on the walls of a cave."

   Find another sentence that Jen wrote that you think is clear, interesting, and complete. Write the sentence here.

   _____

   _____

   _____

Tools & Tips

Your teacher has probably told you that your sentences will be more interesting if you **vary** them. That means making some of your sentences short and some of them long. Here is an example from the selection. Read it out loud. Listen to the rhythm created by the various sentence lengths.

> Soon, one of his students will come into the cave. This boy is different. Old Aknatat can feel it. The boy may be the first Chosen Child in a generation. If he passes the test, Aknatat will start teaching him the special secrets and mysteries that will make him the next Spirit Hunter.

Here is a second example from the reading selection:

> The boy hesitates. Then he touches the wall. Slowly, slowly, he feels the power of the drawings flowing into his fingers.

Read it out loud and listen to the rhythm. Write out the rhythm, using the words **short** and **long** to describe each sentence. Tap out the rhythm, too.

_____

Find another group of sentences in the selection that vary in length. Read them out loud and tap out the rhythm.

Lesson 16

Strategy: Vary Sentence Beginnings

You have practiced two ways to make your sentences more interesting:

✓ Combine sentences.

✓ Vary the sentence length.

Here's a third way:

✓ Vary the sentence beginnings.

Notice how the author of the reading selection *If Walls Could Talk* varies the sentence beginnings:

1. He turns to one charcoal drawing…

2. The dim, dancing light of a torch fire casts the shadow…

3. Before opening it, he lightly touches all the sacred animals…

4. His people hunt these animals for food…

5. Wordlessly, the old man hands the charcoal…

6. Will this one fail, like so many…?

A. How does the beginning of each sentence vary? Discuss with a partner the different ways these sentences begin. For example, which begin with adjectives? Which begin with an adverb? Which begin with a clause? Which begin with the subject?

Identify each sentence beginning, and write your ideas here.

1 _____

_____

2 _____

_____

3 _____

_____

4 _____

_____

5 _____

_____

6 _____

_____

B. Now look at the answer Jen wrote. Find four examples of different ways that she began her sentences.

Write Jen's sentence beginnings here.

1 _____

_____

2 _____

_____

3 _____

_____

4 _____

_____

C. Here are four sentences that all begin the same way. Rewrite each so that it begins in a different way. Use the various sentence openings that both Jen and the author of *If Walls Could Talk* used.

1. A student got on the school bus.

Write your sentence here.

_____

_____

_____

2. She sat down next to me.

Write your sentence here.

_____

_____

_____

3. She looked worried.

Write your sentence here.

_____

_____

_____

4. I wondered what she was thinking.

Write your sentence here.

_____

_____

_____

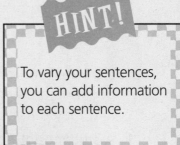

HINT!

To vary your sentences, you can add information to each sentence.

Strategy: Write Extended Answers

One way to write a better answer is to make your answers longer, or extend them. When you answer an open-ended question, the directions often remind you to use details to develop or support your main idea. The easiest way to write an extended answer is to include more details.

To write a really good answer, though, you need to do more than just list details. The details you add should help develop a specific idea. Read the example from Jen's answer. Pay attention to the words in **bold** type:

People don't do **this** today. **They don't make animal drawings on the walls of caves.**

Notice that Jen used the word *this* in the first sentence. You might want to ask, "What don't people do today?" The second sentence answers the question. It tells you what people don't do today.

A. Here is another example from Jen's answer:

A second thing that tells you the story takes place long ago is the kinds of animals in the drawings. There is a wild ox and a giant deer and a mammoth. All the animals in the drawings became extinct thousands of years ago.

1. Which part of the first sentence needs more details?

Write your answer here.

_____

_____

_____

2. What question do you want to ask when you read this sentence?
   Write your answer here.

   _____

   _____

   _____

3. What details does Jen add to answer this question?
   Write your answer here.

   _____

   _____

   _____

   _____

   _____

B. Try it. Here are some general statements about the reading selection. For each one, write a sentence with specific details that answer the question **what** or **why**. Use details from the reading selection.

1. Old Aknatat knows that this boy is different. How is the boy different?
   Write your answer here.

   _____

   _____

   _____

2. The boy stumbles when he enters the cave. Why does the boy stumble?

Write your answer here.

_____

_____

_____

3. It is good that the boy does not cry out. Why is it good?

Write your answer here.

_____

_____

_____

4. The boy feels something when he runs his fingers across the wall. What does the boy feel?

Write your answer here.

_____

_____

_____

5. In his imagination, the boy sees a figure. What figure does he see?

Write your answer here.

_____

_____

_____

Lesson 18

Revising and Improving a Weak Answer

In Lesson 15 you read a good answer to an open-ended question that asked you to read between the lines. You analyzed why it was a good answer. The next step in learning how to write a good answer is to try revising and improving an answer that isn't as successful. Return to *If Walls Could Talk* if you need to.

> **Why doesn't Old Aknatat tell the boy what to draw? Use details from the story to explain your answer.**

Rashid's Answer:

Here is Rashid's answer. It could use some work. Use the questions that follow to help you revise and improve his answer.

> He doesn't tell him what he wants him to draw. The reason is that he wants him to decide for himself what he is going to draw.

Improving Rashid's Answer

Rashid has answered the question:

✓ He has given a reason for Aknatat's behavior.

✓ He has written his answer in complete sentences.

However, Rashid's answer could improve.

✓ His answer is too short.

✓ His first sentence is confusing.

✓ He hasn't included any support details.

Let's work on Rashid's answer. Answer these questions to improve it.

1. Do the two sentences clearly explain the question?

   If not, how can you rewrite the opening? Write a new opening here.

   _____

   _____

   _____

2. Look at paragraph 2 of the story.

Do you see any details in this paragraph that could support Rashid's answer? Write the details here.

_____

_____

_____

3. Find the part in the story where the boy asks, "What do you want me to draw?" Then read Old Aknatat's response and the paragraphs that follow.

Do you see any details that could support Rashid's answer? Write the details here.

_____

_____

_____

4. Look at your answers. Use them to write a better answer to the question.

Write your new answer here.

_____

_____

_____

_____

_____

_____

_____

_____

_____

_____

_____

SCORE BUILDER

Free Writing

Do you have this problem?

Do you get stuck when you have to write?

Do the blank lines seem impossible to fill?

What's the solution?

You may need to practice writing.

How do you do that?

You can practice **free writing**.

Here's how. Write for five minutes—every day if you can. Your teacher will tell you when to begin. Then just write anything that comes into your mind. Don't try to decide whether it's a good idea or not. It is even OK to write "I don't have any ideas" or "I don't know what to write." Just keep moving your pen or pencil, and very soon an idea will come to you. It may not be the best idea in the world— but it will be a beginning.

Responding on Your Own

Now you are going to answer another question about *If Walls Could Talk*. This time you will answer on your own, without models or questions to help you. As you plan and write your answer, think about what you have learned from analyzing Jen's answer and improving Rashid's answer. You should also use the following things to help you write your answer:

✓ the **strategies** you have practiced

✓ the tips you were given in **Tools & Tips**

✓ the reminders in the **Score Builder**

Notice that this question, like the first two, asks you to explain something about the characters and events in the story.

> **Why does Old Aknatat believe that the boy is the "Chosen One"?**
> **Use details from the selection to support your answer.**

Write your answer on the lines below.

_____

_____

_____

_____

_____

_____

_____

HINT!

The test scorers look for the following things:

✳ A clear statement of the answer.

✳ A complete answer to the question.

✳ Details from the story.

✳ Clear, complete, and interesting sentences.

_____

_____

_____

_____

_____

Reader's Response!
Revise & Edit

When you have finished writing, exchange papers with a partner. As you read each other's work, answer the questions below.

1 Did the writer answer the question? ___Yes ___ No

2 Did the writer include enough details from the selection? ___ **Yes** ___ **No**
If not, what needs to be added?
Write your response here.

_____

_____

_____

3 Are the writer's sentences varied and interesting? ___ **Yes** ___ **No**
If not, what needs to be changed?
Write your response here.

_____

_____

_____

4 Has the writer followed all the SLAMS rules? ___ **Yes** ___ **No**
If not, which rules were not followed?
Check all the boxes that apply.

S ___   L ___   A ___   M ___   S ___

5 **Give the paper back to your partner to revise and edit.**

Reviewing the Question

Remember that some questions ask you to read between the lines. This means that they ask you to explain things you need to figure out for yourself. The answers are not stated directly in the text. Instead, you have to look for clues in the text, and **make inferences** based on these clues.

Questions that ask you to make inferences often begin with the question words **how** and **why**. These questions ask you to look at the text more closely and interpret information that is not openly stated. For example:

- **Why** did Jonah slam the door?

- **How** do we know how the character feels?

- **Why** is achieving this task important to the character?

- **How** is the character perceived by others?

- **Why** do the characters react as they do?

- **How** does the character's reaction affect the story?

If a question begins with **how** or **why**, look closely. You might be asked to read between the lines.

Reading Beyond the Lines

Good readers do more than read what is on the page. They do more than read between the lines, too. Good readers also ask themselves questions while they read. They compare the ideas in the text to their own experiences and to what they have observed in the world around them. We call this **reading beyond the lines**.

Sometimes in a reading test you will be asked to read beyond the lines—to add your own thoughts to the ideas presented in the selection.

The next selection is about a girl named Tia whose family decides to read instead of watch TV. The questions that follow are not about the events in the story. Instead, they ask you to make connections between the reading selection and your own ideas and experiences. You need to go beyond what you have read and explain what you think.

Lesson 20

What Makes a Good Answer?

Read the selection below. As you read,
think about your own school.

Pizza and...a Book?

How do Friday nights in the story compare to Friday nights at your home?

Many students in my class have Family Night on Fridays. In my family, that means we get pizza and watch a video. Sometimes we get Chinese food, and sometimes we get burgers, but we always get a movie.

Recently a couple of teachers have been trying to get us to make Friday night Book Night instead of a Movie Night.

Mr. Baker, my teacher, sent home a letter to all the parents. "I encourage everyone to make Friday 'Pizza and a Book Night,'" the letter said. "You can read aloud, read the same book, or read different books. I think you'll find that you will talk about the books with your children. Instead of sitting silently in front of a TV screen, you will find time to communicate with each other. It will improve your child's reading skills as well as the quality of your family time."

I didn't know if I liked the idea, but my parents were excited about it.

"It'll be great," my dad said. "Mom and I can read to you and Steve."

"You haven't read to me since I was tiny!" I said. "I want to rent *Giant Robots Attack!* this Friday."

My dad rolled his eyes and smiled. "It won't be that bad."

On Friday, my mom picked up me and my brother Steve from the after-school program. Normally we would stop by the video store on the way home, but this time we stopped by the library. My little brother picked out *Charlotte's Web*, which I had read the summer before third grade. I picked out a book called *Maniac McGee*, because my mom said it was good and the cover looked cool. We grabbed some pizza on the way home.

What book might you choose?

After dinner we went into the TV room, but we didn't turn on the TV. "Let's read one book out loud for a while before we read our own books," my mom suggested.

"I wanna read *Charlotte's Web*," Steve said, holding the book up. "Can we read this?"

"I've already read it," I said. "Can't we just watch a movie?"

"Tia, let's try reading some of Steve's book," said my dad. "You loved *Charlotte's Web* when you read it."

"Fine." I crossed my arms and sat back on the couch.

My dad picked up *Charlotte's Web*. "No, Dad, I want Tia to read it," said Steve.

"That's a great idea." Dad handed me the book.

I uncrossed my arms and took it. I started to read out loud. *Charlotte's Web* is a story about a talking pig and a spider. I did different voices for the spider and the pig and the girl on the farm. When I got to the end of the first chapter, everyone wanted me to keep reading, so I read Chapter 2, and then Chapter 3. My parents and Steve were laughing at the funny parts, and they liked my voices. I ended up reading five whole chapters. I had forgotten what a good story it is.

When I finished Chapter 5, my mom said, "I'm going to read my book for a while now, but I guess it's OK if you guys watch TV for half an hour."

I started to get up to turn on the TV, but then I said, "Thanks, but I think I want to read my book for a while too." We all sat together. I read *Maniac McGee*, my mom read her book, and my dad read *Charlotte's Web* to Steve. Every once in a while I would ask my mom what a word meant, and a couple of times she read out loud funny things from her book.

When I was going to bed, my mom asked, "So Tia, do you want to rent *Giant Robots Attack!* next Friday?"

"Sure," I said, "but maybe we can watch it on Saturday. Let's save Friday night for reading."

How might you react?

Do you think "Pizza and a Book Night" instead of "Pizza and a Movie Night" is a good idea? Why or why not? Use information from the story and examples from your own experience to support your answer.

Abe's Answer:

Here is Abe's answer. Read what he wrote. Then answer the questions that follow to see what makes Abe's answer so good.

I think it is a good idea to have "Pizza and a Book Night" because that way families spend more time being together and learning together. In the story, Tia doesn't like the idea of reading a book on Friday. She wants to rent a robot movie. But she has a fun time reading <u>Charlotte's Web</u> out loud for her brother. I think that makes her feel proud. By the end of the story, she has changed her mind. She says she wants to read again next Friday.

My mom only lets me and my brother watch TV for half an hour on weeknights. At first we were mad about that, but I think it means we spend more time hanging out together. We play crazy games and sometimes I even read my brother's favorite book to him. That is why "Pizza and a Book Night" is such a good idea.

What Makes Abe's Answer Work?

Abe does all the things that the test scorers look for:

✓ He states his main idea clearly.

✓ He uses details from the selection to back up his opinion.

✓ He uses details from his own experience to explain his answer.

✓ He writes clear and interesting complete sentences.

Now take a closer look at Abe's answer to see what makes it successful.

1. Abe states his main idea in the first paragraph.

   In which sentence does Abe state his main idea? Write Abe's main-idea sentence here.

   _____

   _____

   _____

   _____

2. Abe includes details from the selection to show that he has understood what he has read. He mentions that at first Tia wants to rent a robot movie instead of reading.

   What other details from the selection does he use? Write them here.

   _____

   _____

   _____

   _____

   _____

   _____

   _____

   _____

3. Abe includes his own experiences in his answer. He says that he is only allowed to watch a certain amount of TV.

Find another detail from his own experience that he writes about. Write it here.

_____

_____

_____

_____

4. Abe uses details and examples to support his opinions.

a. **What are Abe's opinions? Write one of Abe's opinions here.**

_____

_____

_____

_____

b. **What kind of support does Abe provide for his opinion? Write a detail or example that Abe uses to support this opinion.**

_____

_____

_____

_____

5. Abe sums up his ideas at the end of his answer.

What is Abe's closing sentence? Write it here.

_____

_____

_____

_____

Tools & Tips

Sometimes, the ideas and events in a story may be very similar to the ways you have felt or things that have happened to you. Other times, the events in the story will remind you of what someone you know has experienced—or even of something you have read or observed around you.

The questions usually ask about situations that will be familiar to you. For example:

> In the story, Sarah Jane worries about what her new school will be like. **Can you remember a time when you or someone you know worried about something new?**

Other selections may focus on things that may be new to you or that you haven't really thought a lot about. If a selection is about divers who explore shipwrecks or about the first flight to the moon, you won't have any direct experience. Don't worry! You still have an imagination. You can use your own experiences and observations to help you imagine what you would do in a new situation.

Try it with this question. Work with a partner to figure out some ways you could answer it.

> In the story, time is running out. Kim has just a few hours to complete his survey of the moon rocks. If something happened, he'd never get back. **Have you ever tried to finish something while "time was running out"? Write about it.**

Lesson 21

Strategy: Adding Details

Read these statements, and try to figure out what's wrong with them.

✓ That book is great.

✓ That movie was silly.

✓ We had a fun time.

✓ She is cool.

Statements like these are important because they state your ideas or opinions. However, they are too general. They need to be supported by details that explain why the book is great or the movie was silly. Adding interesting details to your writing keeps readers interested and helps them understand your ideas.

For example, Morgan wrote this sentence:

My sister is cool.

Morgan's teacher asked her to rewrite the sentence so it included details. Morgan wrote:

My older sister Amanda is cool. She likes really good music, and she shares her stuff with me if I ask her.

The reader gets a better idea of *why* Morgan's sister is cool when Morgan rewrites her sentence and adds details.

What do you know about Morgan's sister and why is she cool? Write your response here.

_____

_____

_____

_____

_____

_____

_____

Read each phrase at the end of the numbered write-on lines. Add a noun before each phrase. A noun is a person, place or thing. Then support your new statement with details.

1 _____ is great.

_____

_____

_____

2 _____ is scary.

_____

_____

_____

3 _____ is my favorite movie.

_____

_____

_____

4 _____ is the best food.

_____

_____

_____

5 _____ was a cool place to go.

_____

_____

_____

Lesson 22

Strategy: Using Examples

Using examples from your own experiences shows the reader that you have made connections between the story and your own life. A good example also makes your writing come alive. Read the paragraph below. Indira wanted to explain why she thinks it's important to help other people.

It is important to help other people. If you help someone, they will be ready to help you if you need them. Last fall, I helped my neighbor Sam rake all the leaves in his yard. He was really happy that I helped him. This winter, when my mom asked me to shovel the walk up to our house, Sam helped me. It went quicker because Sam helped, and we drank hot chocolate afterward.

Try it. Practice using examples from your own experiences.

1. Think of an example from your own experiences that will explain why it is important to help other people.

Write your response here.

_____

_____

_____

_____

_____

_____

_____

2. Choose one of the following statements as the first sentence in a paragraph. Circle the sentence. Then complete the paragraph by writing an example that supports or explains the statement.

✓ Playing sports teaches you how to get along with other people.

✓ Reading a book can help expand your imagination.

✓ My friends have taught me important things.

Write your response here.

_____

_____

_____

_____

_____

_____

_____

_____

_____

_____

_____

_____

_____

_____

_____

_____

_____

_____

HINT!

Think about your own experiences, things that have happened to friends, or stories that you have read or seen on TV.

Lesson 23

Revising and Improving a Weak Answer

The next step in learning how to write a good answer is revising and improving an answer that isn't successful. Read the question below. Notice that this question also asks you to include your own experiences to support your answer.

> **In the story, Tia doesn't want to read instead of watching videos, but by the end of the story she has changed her mind. Can you think of a time when you weren't excited about doing something, but you ended up enjoying it? How was your experience like Tia's? Support your answer with details from the story and from your own experience.**

Jordan's Answer:

Read Jordan's answer carefully. Then use the questions that follow to help you revise and improve his answer.

> Tia changed her mind about reading. I used to think basketball was boring, but now I think it's cool. My brother is awesome at basketball. He's good at football, too. Then I learned to play, and I found out basketball is great.

Improving Jordan's Answer

Jordan has begun to answer the question.

✓ He has stated his opinion.

✓ He has used an example from his own life to back up his opinion.

But Jordan's answer needs work:

✓ It is too short.

✓ It doesn't include many details or examples from the story or from Jordan's own life.

✓ Jordan has used the words *cool* and *great* without explaining what he means.

✓ Even though all his sentences are complete, some of them do not relate to his answer.

Let's revise and improve Jordan's answer.

1. Jordan writes that Tia changed her mind about reading.

   What details from the story can we add to explain Tia's experience in more depth? Write the new sentence with details from the story here.

   _____

   _____

   _____

2. Jordan writes that he used to think basketball was boring, but now he thinks basketball is cool and great.

   What example might Jordan use from his own life to explain "cool" and "great"? Write the example here.

   _____

   _____

   _____

3. Two of Jordan's sentences do not relate to his answer. They do not help the reader understand why his experience is like Tia's.

   Which two sentences should be deleted? Write the sentences here.

   _____

   _____

   _____

4. Jordan needs a strong closing sentence.

   How can Jordan sum up his experience and how it compares to Tia's experience? Write a closing sentence here.

   _____

   _____

   _____

SCORE BUILDER

When you use examples from your own experiences, make sure you stay on topic. Do not change the subject and start writing about something that is unrelated to the question.

1. Read the following paragraph and decide which sentence is "off topic."

> My neighbor Darcy is going to be a great artist. She can draw and paint. She used to always draw with chalk on the sidewalk when we were little. She moved to my neighborhood when she was five, and she has two brothers. She also makes pretty paintings that she gives to me on my birthday.

Write the sentence that does not belong in this paragraph.

_____

_____

_____

2. Read these sentences. Which sentence would best replace the sentence that doesn't belong? **Circle it.**

Darcy has a hamster and a cat.

All the neighbors thought Darcy's chalk drawings were great.

Darcy is really tall with dark hair.

3. **Explain why the sentence you picked fits best.**

_____

_____

_____

Responding On Your Own

Now you are going to answer another question about the story *Pizza and...a Book?* This time you will answer on your own, without models or questions to help you. As you plan and write your answer, think about what you have learned from analyzing Abe's successful answer and improving Jordan's weak answer. You should also use the following to help write your answer:

✓ the **strategies** you have practiced

✓ the tips you were given in **Tools & Tips**

✓ the reminders in the **Score Builder**

> **How would you convince a friend to have "Pizza and a Book Night" instead of "Pizza and a Movie Night"? Write a letter to a friend. Explain why you think "Pizza and a Book Night" is a good idea. Support your idea with details from the story and from your own life.**

Write your answer on the lines below.

_____

_____

_____

_____

_____

_____

_____

_____

_____

_____

_____

_____

HINT!

Test scorers look for the following things:

✴ A clear statement of your opinion.

✴ A complete answer to the question.

✴ Details from the story and from your own experience.

✴ Clear, complete, and interesting sentences.

Reader's Response!
Revise & Edit

When you have finished writing, exchange papers with a partner. As you read each other's answers, follow these steps:

1 Do you think the writer clearly stated the main idea?   ___Yes ___ No
If not, what needs to be added or changed?

Write your response here.

_____

_____

_____

2 Has the writer included supporting details from   ___ Yes ___ No
the text and from his or her own experience?
If not, what needs to be added or changed?

Write your response here.

_____

_____

_____

3 Was the writer's personal experience   ___ Yes ___ No
convincing? If not, what needs to be added or changed?

Write your response here.

_____

_____

_____

4 Has the writer followed all the SLAMS rules?   ___ Yes ___ No
If not, which rules were not followed?

Check all the boxes that apply.

S ___   L ___   A ___   M ___   S ___

5 **Give the paper back to your partner to revise and edit.**

Reviewing the Question

Remember that a question that asks you to read beyond the lines is asking you to **make connections**. You should make connections to:

- your own experiences

- the world around you

The point of the reading selection is to provide you with a subject and some information. The main idea of the selection becomes a springboard for your own ideas. Test questions that ask you to read beyond the lines may be phrased in the following ways:

- Tell about an experience you had that is similar to the one in the selection.

- Imagine how you would react in a similar situation.

- Explain if you agree or disagree with the ideas posed in the selection.

Read this selection. Then answer the questions that follow.

Write Me!

Cassie paused at the door to her cousin's room.

"Go ahead," her mother said. "I'll wait out here."

Last year, Cassie's cousin Meredith had moved with her family across the country to California. Only a few weeks after the move, Cassie was riding her bike when she was hit by a truck and badly injured. Cassie and Meredith were almost the same age and best friends, and now Meredith might never walk or talk again.

The first time Cassie visited Meredith after the accident, Meredith was in a coma. Seeing Meredith surrounded by beeping, hissing machines was scary. Meredith had been so lively, and she loved to laugh. Meredith's mother suggested that Cassie talk to Meredith "like normal." Cassie tried, but it was hard without hearing Meredith talk back. There was nothing normal about it.

Nearly a year had gone by. Meredith was now in a rehabilitation center. Cassie took a deep breath and walked into the room.

"Hello," said a woman sitting beside Meredith. "You must be Cassie. Meredith's been expecting you."

Meredith lay flat in bed, like the last time Cassie had seen her. This time, though, Meredith's eyes were open and alert. She looked at Cassie, and her look seemed to say, "Hello!"

"My name is Donna," the woman said. "I'm Meredith's speech therapist. She told me you're her favorite cousin."

Cassie smiled, leaned down, and hugged Meredith, then she sat in a chair by the bed. She noticed a computer screen off to the side. Donna was adjusting something near Meredith's feet.

Drawn by Donna's movement, Cassie watched, fascinated, as Meredith's right foot began to move back and forth on an electronic board at the foot of the bed. Letters appeared in boxes on a computer screen, and they shifted with each tap of Meredith's foot. As soon as a letter lit up, it joined others at the top of the screen: HI CASS.

Cassie stared at Meredith, whose eyes gleamed back, as if smiling.

"Wow! You're…Hi! Wow!" was all Cassie could say. Meredith's foot tapped again. The movements were slow and shaky, and Donna had to hold the board steady for her. Meredith's big toe strained to push the buttons. HOW IS OSCAR?

Cassie's eyes pricked with happy tears. Oscar was her dog. "He's good!" she told her cousin. "He loves California! The other day he caught a lizard. Mom freaked out!" She was sure Meredith's eyes were smiling.

"Her feet are touching 'intellikeys,'" Donna explained to her. "She chooses the letters one at a time. She's a good speller."

LAKE SOON.

"I don't know if we're going this year," Cassie said in response. Meredith and Cassie's family had vacationed together many times at the lake. "Your dad says he needs to stay around here."

Meredith's eyes looked sad for a moment.

"Don't worry, we'll get back to the lake someday," Cassie said. "Remember Alex? He had a crush on you."

A word appeared on the computer screen: CUTE.

Cassie and Meredith continued to communicate in this way until Cassie's mother arrived.

HI AUNT PEG Meredith typed.

Cassie's mother was amazed.

Cassie laughed. "Pretty neat, huh? Donna says we might be able to e-mail each other, too."

"That's right," Donna agreed. "We can hook the communication device up to a computer and send e-mails."

Eventually, it was time to leave. Cassie hugged her cousin, trying hard not to cry. As she went through the door, she turned around. "Write me, okay?"

Meredith's gaze lit up the room.

1 Reading What Is on the Page

What changes did Meredith go through between Cassie's visits? Use details from the selection in your answer.

_____

_____

_____

_____

_____

_____

_____

_____

_____

_____

_____

_____

_____

_____

_____

_____

_____

_____

_____

2 Reading Between the Lines

What is communication, and why is it so important to Meredith and Cassie? Use details from the selection and your own ideas in your answer.

_____

_____

_____

_____

_____

_____

_____

_____

_____

_____

_____

_____

_____

_____

_____

_____

_____

_____

_____

_____

3 Reading Beyond the Lines

What other ways do people have to communicate besides writing and speaking? Use details from the selection and your own ideas, experiences, and observations to answer the question.

_____

_____

_____

_____

_____

_____

_____

_____

_____

_____

_____

_____

_____

_____

_____

_____

_____

_____

_____

_____